No Holds Barred

*

IVOR BIGG-WIGG QC

Published in 1992 by Stag Publications
16 Connaught Street, Marble Arch,
London W2 2AF
Telephone: 071-724 7748
Fax: 071-724 5766 Telex: 299067

ISBN 0-9518669-0-7

Cartoons, Chris McAllen
Cover design, Caradus

Printed on re-tree economy paper by Booksprint,
017/31 Clerkenwell Close, London EC1R 0AT

To Sally

The author wishes to thank his wife Sally for keeping the children at bay whilst this book was being written, and to Jane King for her patient proof reading and helpful suggestions.

Any resemblance between characters in this book and real persons, dead or still living, is entirely deliberate.

Introduction

THIS HUMOROUS and lighthearted book examines a jury trial set in any one of the innumerable Crown Courts which pepper these sceptred isles (with the obvious exceptions of Scotland and Northern Ireland, where they like to do their own thing), as seen through the eyes of the defence advocate. It takes you, the reader, through the criminal process from the moment the advocate first meets the accused, to glorious acquittal, or sometimes, sadly, to conviction and sentence.

Crime and punishment continue to hold an almost morbid fascination for the public at large, and everybody has an opinion to offer on the burning issue of the day. Topical issues such as rape, child abuse and the hardy perennial of capital punishment all vie for space in the tabloids and the media until more controversial issues replace them. The criminal law is also a topic of lively debate at all levels of society, as one interest group or another voices its support, or criticism, of the various legal institutions from the police constable on the beat to the loftiest legal luminaries in the land, who, in their glorious isolation in the Court of Appeal or the House of Lords, cannot, or should not, be immune to the slings and arrows of outraged misfortune.

The government of Margaret Thatcher, for good reasons no doubt, sought to break the monopoly of the Bar to practise exclusively in the higher courts, and in spite of much vocal opposition and self flagellation, the solicitor advocate will emerge from his chrysalis to flutter onto the stage and into the limelight. Whether or not this is in the interests of justice, only time will tell.

This book does not pretend to address itself to these and other issues which will preoccupy the experts, real or imagined, for some time to come. It focuses instead on the sharp end of the criminal law as a civilised society goes about the Queen's business in search of truth and justice. It strips away the mystique surrounding the law, as it lifts the veil on all the pomp and ceremony, and exposes a lot of the humbug that bedevils a profession which many believe is still ossified in the nineteenth century. But it doesn't end there. It gives a penetrating insight into the roles of the various players in the drama as it unfolds, and their respective functions and contributions.

Finally, it takes a critical look at the role of the Judge in the proceedings, the central figure in the drama who has enormous power to control and influence the outcome of the trial. Whether or not that power is excessive, or is wielded in the interests of justice, is another matter. As to that, the jury are still out.

Contents

CHAPTER ONE

The Accused

GENERALLY SPEAKING, he will be as thick as two short planks, and on legal aid, a most unattractive combination. It's a fact of life that the rich and successful very rarely get prosecuted, and if they do, they wheel on the heavyweight luminaries of the legal profession to bamboozle the jury and suck up to the judge. Assume therefore that your client, the accused, has none of these obvious advantages, and will start with one grave disadvantage, namely that as he's in the dock, he must be guilty of something.

His appearance will be depressing, even if he's put on his best suit for the occasion. If he's young, he will almost certainly have some sort of ornament in his ear, and probably a whole collection. If you're lucky, his tattoos will be discreetly hidden, along with the more offensive messages contained thereon. If you're not, he'll have a thundering great tattoo right in the middle of his forehead with the cryptic message "Stuff the Pigs" surrounded by snakes. Try not to stare, it only makes things worse!

You will be expected to 'take instructions' from this creature of the black lagoon. This means, in short, that you will have to listen to his side of the story. If you are a solicitor, then you will invite him to your office for a chat, and you will be prepared for the mountain you will have to climb when his trial begins. If you are a barrister, or 'counsel' as you will be known to one and all, to your face at least, then you may not have met your client until you get to court, and there is little that can be done to prepare you for the shock. You will have to grin and bear it!

Your client, particularly the tattooed and bejewelled variety, will almost certainly have been charged under one or more of the panaceaic public order offences so favoured by the police and the more aggressive members of the Crown Prosecution Service. He instructs you that he is not guilty, so the first thing to do is to examine the strength of the evidence against him. Let's assume, for the sake of illustration, that your client, paralytically drunk, has emerged from the Cock and Bull Public House on a Friday night at closing time with a group of his chums, singing a well known refrain which he'd learned over the years, one line at a time, on the terraces of his local football club. The prosecution eye witnesses will describe how the youth with the thundering great tattoo in the middle of his forehead, aided and abetted by his drunken companions, attacked a group of innocent bystanders, all to a man and woman perfectly respectable middle class model citizens (they invariably are!), kicking out and punching as many as were in range. The police are called, and at least half a dozen boys in blue will give evidence that they saw, amongst others, your client doing exactly that, and when challenged, he struggled violently and had to be restrained. This is a police euphemism for the same half dozen officers piling on top of your client, giving him the good kicking he richly deserves, handcuffing him, and then tossing him, like a sack of potatoes, into the back of a transit van, with just enough force to avoid serious injury or the need to call the police doctor. After documentation at the police station, he will be interviewed in the absence of a solicitor, (to be explained later), and he will have made a full confession to the crimes with which he is later charged, and to make matters worse, he will have signed it.

The charges will reflect the numbers game. If your client is charged alone, then affray will fit the bill, with a couple of random assaults thrown in for good measure. If he is charged together with his companions, then violent disorder will be plucked from the statute book. If he's one of a larger number of miscreants, he'll be charged with riot.

There are basically two approaches when faced with this sort of evidence. The first, for the fainthearted, is to tell your client, regardless of what he says, that the evidence is overwhelming, that he's bound to be convicted by the jury, and he might as well plead guilty and take the consequences. But this is hardly the way to hone your skills as an advocate to a razor sharp cutting edge. Your reputation will be made in the face of adversity, not by caving in at the first obstacle. And anyway, there is always a remote possibility that your client is innocent of the charges, although, it has to be admitted, it's remote in the extreme.

Not then for you the easy option, or the cut and run approach. From little acorns, mighty oaks do grow, and there's always a chance that half the jury have previous convictions for doing exactly the same thing, so there's a fairly sizeable sympathy vote to start with!

Let us assume, therefore, that you decide to grasp the nettle and prepare your client's case for trial. You will listen patiently to his explanations, resisting the temptation to laugh out loud. You will carefully consider the eye witness accounts, and you will be comforted in the knowledge that several months will elapse between the date of the incident and the beginning of the trial. The longer the time gap between these two events, the more their evidence becomes a test of memory, and the more witnesses there are, the greater the possibility of inconsistencies in their respective accounts which you, as the skilled advocate, will pounce upon and rattle like a sabre in front of the jury. The thundering great tattoo right in the middle of your client's forehead is a considerable millstone around your neck, if you'll forgive the mixed metaphors, so if you can find two or three yobs similarly disfigured to sit in the front row of the public gallery, snorting ostentatiously and wiping their noses on the back of their hands, then so much the better. It's a long shot, but worth considering.

Your client's instructions on the police evidence will be less farcical, and probably true. He will almost certainly tell you that after he had been dragged unceremoniously from the back of the transit van and dumped into a urine drenched cell with fourteen other inmates, he was visited from time to time, just as he was dozing off, and asked if he wanted a solicitor present during interview. Being street wise, he will say yes, which will produce snorts of derision and lots of shaking of heads. After about eight hours in custody, he will be told that he can wait for another three days whilst attempts are made to contact a solicitor, or alternatively, if he is willing to waive that right, he can be interviewed there and then and be on his way home in an hour. Being human, just, he will eventually agree, and the interview can begin.

The police officers will record the interview on paper, as they are required to do, and at the conclusion, your client will be shown where to sign and initial the record as being true, and then, with everything nicely stitched up, he will either be packed off into the cold night air or banged up in the cells again to await his first appearance at the local magistrates court. Promises are like pie crusts, easily broken.

The skilled advocate will always ask for his client's custody record, which is filled in with varying degrees of accuracy whilst he is detained at the police station. In most cases, that record is disclosed by the Crown Prosecution Service (CPS), as late as possible before trial if at all, and it can sometimes make interesting reading.

You could pick up a clue or two to support your client's version of events, but don't bet your life on it!

As a solicitor advocate, you will then take your client's proof of evidence, which is his version of events, and will have to chase up any leads which he might give you. As a barrister advocate, you will expect all this to be done for you, but you will sometimes be disappointed.

The barrister advocate will often be advised to hold a conference with the client, assuming of course that he gets the brief to represent him in good time. Briefs have a habit of appearing on the night before the trial, which severely limits the advocate's scope for original thought.

Conferences are held by convention in the barrister's chambers. If in London, these chambers are usually housed in ramshackle, dilapidated buildings in the Temple, dating from the eighteenth century with furnishings and electrical fittings to match. The client will be making his own way, so expect him to be anything between half an hour and an hour late. As his advocate, your client will expect you to be unbelievably pompous, which happily comes easily to most barristers. If you are not pompous by nature, then you should work on it, as the client will expect lofty phrases like 'burden and standard of proof', and 'mens rea' peppering the conference, even though he doesn't understand a word of it.

Try not to depress him too much. His defence may be laughable, but telling him that securing an acquittal is equivalent to scaling the north face of the Eiger without oxygen will do little for his morale, and may shake his confidence in you. And don't forget, try not to stare!

The conference over, you are now ready for trial, or as ready as you ever will be! But take heart, the worst is yet to come!

CHAPTER TWO

Foreplay

THE BIG DAY has finally arrived, and you travel to court with a mounting sense of dread. Wrong! Positive thought is what is wanted now, and unless you exude confidence from the first bell, you may find yourself on the ropes before you've emerged from your corner.

The preliminary skirmishes, or foreplay, are about to begin, as you studiously ignore your client and make your way to the robing room. If you are a solicitor, you will have your own quarters set apart from those reserved for barristers. In the new order of things, these niceties of rank and privilege will become blurred and eventually erode, but for the time being, hang on to what you've got. Your room will be larger, more spacious, and better equipped than the barristers robing room, and the ablutions will accommodate at least four standing shoulder to shoulder. If your opponent is also a solicitor on the CPS payroll, so much the better, as he will be as nervous as a kitten, and looking to you to throw him a lifeline. Do no such thing! Your task at the outset is to rubbish his case and keep him on edge.

Like a matador, you must compose yourself as you don your 'suit of lights'. This consists of a wing collar and bands, in the way of things ecclesiastical, and a gown. If you are a barrister, you will top off this ludicrous ensemble with an uncomfortable horsehair wig. Wigs are still favoured by a minority of unenlightened barristers as the hallmark of their profession and distinguish them from other, better paid, professionals who occasionally tread the legal boards. As the cost of a wig increases in adverse proportion to a barrister's earnings, a number of highly stylized models have appeared on the market. But a word of advice to the newly called barristers amongst you. New looking wigs are extremely unfashionable, and label you as a beginner. To avoid being tarred with this brush by your fellow professionals, see if you can buy an old one from somebody who's been elevated to one of a number of judicial or quasi-judicial posts on offer, or better still, somebody who's seen the error of his ways, jacked it in and become a market gardener. This wig will be old and grey, preferably torn in several places, sweat stained and an obvious health hazard. If you can't find an old one, then try and age your new one by using it to clean the car, or tie it to the exhaust and drive up to Cumberland, or throw it up into the air and shoot at it with your grandfather's twelve bore, or preferably, all three.

Whilst the legal profession remains firmly rooted in the Middle Ages, proper court dress is still strictly observed, and your judge may be a stickler for convention. Avoid the fluorescent shirt or the lightweight shiny Italian suit, otherwise he may not be able to 'hear you'. This expression has caused confusion and not a little embarrassment when used by judges in open court. If your attire falls below the standards adopted by funeral directors for their most favoured clients, then the judge, instead of simply telling you that he doesn't approve, will tell you that he can't hear you. Now this remark requires some pretty fast thinking, particularly if the remark comes early in the trial before you've had a chance to weigh him up. He could be referring to your attire, equally, he could be some old buffer working out his final years before retirement who's actually as deaf as a post. So the best advice is to smile indulgently and shout at the top of your voice. If he smiles back and nods appreciatively, then you know you've got a deaf one. He may, however, shake his head disapprovingly, without actually resolving your dilemma. Like the Mousetrap, this particular farce could run and run, and there are no hard and fast rules for resolving it. If you'll forgive the pun, you'll have to play it by ear, but such a performance is most distracting when you should be concentrating all your energies and resources on the task ahead. The best advice is to avoid any possible confrontation by dressing soberly and conservatively.

But enough of these unwelcome distractions! Back to the robing room!

After you've donned your 'suit of lights', and composed yourself, you're ready for the foreplay. Begin by identifying your opposite number. If he's equally well versed in the art of foreplay, he'll tell you he's prepared the case for plea, as your client has no defence whatsoever. This is a strong opening gambit, called the Queen's Gambit, as he prosecutes on behalf of the Crown. But don't let him upset you. Tell him you thought he'd be offering no evidence. This will throw him off balance, although he'll try not to show it:

"You're joking of course! The case against your client is overwhelming!"

To which you reply:

"I'm amazed to hear you say that. Your main eye witness certainly doesn't share your confidence."

With that, you wheel majestically away and out of the robing room, leaving your opponent with a rising sense of panic. You'll not see him again for at least another thirty minutes, as he pores over his eye witness's account line by line, over and over again. First round to you!

You are now ready to meet your client, and a few minutes spent holding his hand will help comfort him enormously. This is the opportunity to go over a few points about the mechanics of the trial. If you are Counsel, then you may be accompanied by a solicitor's representative, who will know nothing about the case whatsoever. Many can be best described as 'outdoor clerks', who are retired gentlefolk tempted back into the market place with the offer of twenty pounds a day and the chance to doze peacefully in a warm Crown Court. They will pick up the case file from the solicitor's office on the morning of the trial, and meet the client and his barrister at court. Thereafter, their main task will be to note what time they arrive at court, and when they leave, so that the solicitor can claim their expenses at the end of each working day.

The pretrial conference at court should be as short as possible, mainly because you won't get paid for it. It is also another useful gambit in the foreplay game, to allow your opponent to reflect upon your opening skirmishes, and to discover that half his witnesses haven't as yet turned up. This heightens the tension, and places you firmly in the driving seat.

After a few brief pleasantries with your client, you are ready for round two.

You will find your opponent in anxious conversation with the clerk from the CPS. She, for they are invariably female, is the prosecution equivalent of the solicitor's representative, and she too will know nothing about the case. Her task is to ensure that the prosecuting barrister does nothing without the permission of the CPS 'vetting' solicitor. Regardless of his experience as an advocate, the prosecuting counsel will have to refer all decisions through her to this mysterious character, who is never seen at court, but who decides, from the comfort of his civil service regulation office several miles away, exactly how the case should proceed. It is important for the defence advocate to remember this rather curious command structure, especially during foreplay, for obvious reasons. Your opponent may come up to you with a perfectly acceptable offer which your client may be foolish to refuse. But don't forget, he's got to sell it to his 'vetting' solicitor, who may take a totally different view of the matter, and send him back into court with a smacked wrist and the implied threat of no more work unless he bucks up his ideas. It's called having a dog and barking yourself.

The second round of foreplay is called plea bargaining. Your opening gambit may have shaken your opponent's confidence in his case, but perhaps not fatally so. He will open the bidding:

"I'm prepared to take a magnanimous view, although I still think I've got a watertight case against your client..."

Already the signs of nagging doubt, as the seeds you planted earlier begin to take root...

"...so I'll consider a plea to a lesser charge and drop the more serious charge."

You snort derisively. "My dear chap," you reply in your most patronising voice, "you've got no case and you know it." (A monumental overstatement, but so what?) "But I'll tell you what I might do. You offer no evidence, and my client may be willing to be bound over."

You see in his eyes that flicker of hope as your opponent wrestles with his conscience but then it is gone. The shadow of the 'vetting' solicitor looms over him, and that haunted, hunted look returns. His shoulders sag with resignation.

"There's no point discussing the matter further. We'll have to let the jury decide."

“Quite so,” you reply affably, “and I’m confident they’ll reach the right verdict.”

A nice little parting shot, as he slopes off. So ends the foreplay. Now to the serious business in hand!

COURT ONE

CHAPTER THREE

Dramatis Personae

THE USHER

YOUR CASE is called on, literally, from the door of the court, by one of the ushers, usually of the female persuasion. These raddled harridans have been recruited from the major seaports around the country where they were earning a living of sorts as fishwives, in order to shout the odds in court. Beware! They must be handled with extreme caution. Many an advocate has come seriously unstuck by failing to comment in glowing terms upon their latest hairdo, or to congratulate one of their number upon the expected happy event. But don't just blunder in! She may simply have put on a lot of weight since you last saw her, and your congratulations will almost certainly give offence.

Besides shouting the odds, they have a variety of other tasks to perform. They can best be described as 'gophers'. They will be delegated to go and fetch the judge from his room once the court has assembled, or distribute documents to the jury, or hand up exhibits to a witness. These little tasks, so important to the smooth running of a crown court, are carried out with varying degrees of enthusiasm and efficiency during the course of the trial. Happily, there is always time for a little nap during the course of the day, or a stab at the *Daily Mirror* crossword.

The experienced advocate will choose his moment carefully before calling upon the usher to perform some menial task. It should either be as early as possible in the morning session, or immediately after lunch when the court reassembles, and when the usher will be as alert as she ever will be. Thereafter, she will rapidly lose interest, and you disturb her at her peril.

There are two other important reasons why the usher should be handled with kid gloves. Many have been ushering the same judge in and out of court for years, and they have obviously built up a considerable rapport. Putting in a good word for you can work wonders, and the judge will be all smiles every time you rise to your feet. But a bad word can mean the kiss of death!

Additionally, the usher will double as jury bailiff. This rather lofty title confers upon her the task of mothering the jury and presiding over their deliberations when they retire to consider their verdict. She will therefore be in intimate contact with the twelve honest and upright citizens who will be trying your case, and the longer it goes on, the more intimate the contact. In their turn, the members of the jury look to her for guidance and comfort in strange surroundings, where they will feel like new pupils on their first day at school, and the usher fills the role of surrogate Matron. She will exchange pleasantries with them several times a day, as they troop in and out of court with monotonous regularity. She will chat to them in the privacy of their room, making sure they've all been to the lavatory before coming into court, that they have paper and pencils to make notes during the trial, (to be discouraged if at all possible, but sometimes unavoidable), and if they have any questions, they will ask her. She, at her discretion, will then decide if any matters should be referred to the judge.

When the jury retire to consider their verdict, she will escort them to their retiring room and settle them in. She will arrange sandwiches and coffee, and then park herself outside their door as their deliberations get under way. If the jury have any problems, they will knock on their door, and the same usher will open it and give what assistance she can. Only in extremis will she feel the need to get a second opinion, so she wields enormous power, and you mustn't forget it!

THE COURT CLERK

Next in order of importance is the court clerk. She is invariably of the female persuasion, although one or two men have squeezed through the net. She is the majordomo or mistress of ceremonies, and conducts the formalities throughout the trial. Her specific task will be examined in detail during the trial itself, but in general terms, she is the judge's mouthpiece in court, just as the usher is his mouthpiece out of court.

In days of yore, the court clerk was often a qualified barrister who, for one reason or another, had eschewed the heady world of private practice and settled himself comfortably into the less remunerative, but cosier, career as one of the Lord Chancellor's minions. However, the civil service, for ever jealous of its powers and privileges, soon put a stop to that, and without a union card, the barrister was frozen out. This heralded the advent of the undiluted civil servant.

Court clerks are now plucked from a variety of backgrounds and work experience, but the most favoured training ground is the typing pool of the DHSS.

The court clerk's attendance in court is indispensable at the beginning of the trial, as she it is who decides when the proceedings can commence. Again, like the usher, you must have careful regard for her feelings, and, like most prima donnas, she can be notoriously temperamental and quickly turn hostile. Once the proceedings are under way, her attendance thereafter is sporadic in the extreme, as she busies herself with other duties of an indeterminate nature, like ordering the coffee and tea for the clerks' room, and making sure that enough supplies of fresh milk are delivered daily. This means that she can never be found when she's needed, an essential qualification for a good civil servant.

Failure to humour her can cause all sorts of problems which you'd rather be without. She has sole access to the court file, and its accompanying documents and reports, which you may need to smooth you along the way. If she's feeling particularly contrary towards you, she will refuse your request to have a short chat with your bemused client, or worse still, you've just purchased an incredibly expensive and revolting cup of coffee from the vending machine when you're called back into court.

But most important of all, the court clerk will be responsible for paying the pitiful fees you will receive several months after the conclusion of the trial. When you gasp in shock horror at the fees allowed, seeing but not believing, you will ask that same court clerk to redetermine them. Several weeks after that, she will refuse to increase them, and accompany her refusal with a well directed raspberry!

THE LOGGER

The logger is the natural successor to the shorthand writer or stenographer, the keeper of the court record, and another brainchild of the civil service. Again, like the usher and the court clerk, the logger is usually of the female persuasion, giving rise to a serious debate about equality of opportunity in the work place.

Not so long ago, the extremely proficient shorthand writer or stenographer was responsible for keeping a verbatim record of the court proceedings. It was a highly skilled task, requiring great speed and accuracy, and it worked very well. If there was a query about what a witness had said, it could be resolved immediately and the verbatim record read back to the court. Because it worked so well, the civil service decided to change it. But more importantly, most of the shorthand writers and stenographers were employed by private firms, and yes, you've guessed it, they didn't have a union card!

So the Lord Chancellor's department, (equipment, the acquisition of), hit upon a brilliant idea. They decided to tape record the court proceedings, and immediately ordered and installed several thousand tape recorders in every court in the land, along with several thousand microphones strategically placed around the court to catch every spoken word. But just in case the recorder malfunctioned, it was further decided to buy and install several thousand back up recorders, so now every court in the land has two. But of course, the tape recorder has to be switched on and off so the redundant shorthand writers and stenographers were dragooned in to operate them at great expense. Finally, as if this were not enough, these highly trained and proficient operatives are required to make a log of the proceedings, hence their title. Basically, this consists of a sheet of paper, onto which is logged the salient moments of the unfolding drama. For example:

10.32 am—Judge enters court.
10.35 am—Prosecution Counsel addresses court.
11.15 am—Ten minute break to relieve the boredom.

In the way of things mechanical, these recorders sometimes develop a mind of their own, and during particularly boring passages of evidence, they will emit whines and low moans like tortured souls from the depths of hell. This is the signal for total confusion as the entire proceedings grind to a halt. The logger knows nothing about the way in which these machines function, so she is resigned to smiling nervously and colouring visibly. Inconsiderate judges will simply sit tight and wait for the problem to be resolved, others will slope off to their rooms and read the newspaper, or perhaps have a stab at the *Daily Mirror* crossword. The Courts Administrator has not as yet taken a logger technician onto the payroll, but it can only be a matter of time, so in the case of a particularly stubborn machine, there is no alternative but to remove it from court in disgrace, and bring in a replacement. Fortunately, every court has a store of yet more, backup machines, purchased with commendable foresight for just such an emergency, so no more than an hour of court time is lost whilst the replacement is requisitioned from the stores, brought into court, wired up, and checked, and the appropriate entry is made on the log.

THE JURY

Twelve honest men and true, was how they used to be described in less enlightened times, but that bears no resemblance to the modern jury. The days when the jury was composed of male adult ratepayers have long since gone, for better or for worse. Nowadays the qualifications are far less restricted. The age limit has been lowered to eighteen, and both sexes are equally represented.

Usually, potential jurors are drawn from the court's local catchment area, but not necessarily. Some crown courts find themselves in relatively deprived urban areas, where it is often difficult to distinguish between jurors and the accused. Convictions were such a rarity that it was decided to widen the catchment area in the hope of attracting a more prosecution minded jury, but this has met with only limited success. The shire counties have less of a problem, as respectability and prejudice often go hand in hand.

When summoned for jury service, Joe Public has little comprehension of what is in store for him. He will know that he's expected to make himself available for two weeks, and he will labour under the misguided belief that he's going to sit on a jury. He will rapidly be disabused of both misconceptions. He may find himself selected to sit on a jury for a trial estimated to last six weeks, and unless he can show good cause for being excused, he's lumbered. So much for his two week stint! But at least he's being gainfully employed, even if it's for longer than his worst nightmare. But so many trials never get started, for one reason or another, that most jurors spend their two weeks sitting alongside a ragbag collection of total strangers, crowded into the jury assembly room hour after hour, with nothing to do but smoke, strike up a random conversation, or stare aimlessly out of the window. After the third day, the more literary inclined will arm themselves with blockbuster novels, whilst those less erudite will struggle manfully with the *Daily Mirror* crossword.

THE JUDGE

In the not too dim and distant past, when advocates had come to the end of their useful professional shelf life, they were appointed judges. This meant that they were invariably in the twilight of their years, with all the disabilities of old age, hard of hearing, intolerant, and often incontinent. But more recently, the Lord Chancellor's department (Judges, the acquisition of), has opted for younger, more durable material, together with the index linked pension.

The first thing for the advocate to remember is that the judge considers himself to be terribly important, regardless of his age and experience, and will expect everybody to behave accordingly. This will mean a tremendous amount of bowing and scraping, and the use of deferential language at all times. There are basically three types of judge found lurking at the crown court.

THE HIGH COURT JUDGE

The High Court Judge is very important indeed, and is addressed by all and sundry as 'My Lord'. He wears a red gown trimmed with ermine, which makes him look like a rather grumpy pantomime Dame. He visits the crown court from time to time, as the Lord Chancellor's department (Judges, the movement of) determines, and he's accompanied by much pageant and ceremony. In fact, it's a little bit like a travelling Fred Karno's Circus come to town, with trumpeters to sound a fanfare when he comes into court, accompanied by a rather comic character dressed like a floor walker at Fortnum and Mason's, a smattering of local dignitaries with a mace and a sword or two, and to complete the spectacle, caged animals brought up from the dungeons to entertain the assembled multitude.

High Court Judges, because they are very important indeed, usually have the most serious cases reserved to them, so that they can pass outrageously savage sentences in keeping with their importance and the expectations of right minded readers of the more popular tabloids. It sometimes happens that the most serious cases are exhausted before the Judge's tour of duty comes to an end, and it has been known for the occasional bemused and shell-shocked shoplifter to find himself hauled up and sent down before his feet can touch the ground. Probation and Community Service haven't yet found their way into the High Court Judge's vocabulary.

THE CIRCUIT JUDGE

The Circuit Judge is next in order of importance. He, or very occasionally she, is the regular, full time crown court judge, handling the run of the mill crown court workload. He will be regaled in an absolutely ghastly multicoloured gown, and will be addressed as 'Your Honour'.

Unlike the High Court Judge, who rarely touches base with the common herd, the circuit judge usually stays put

in one crown court. This of course provides fertile ground for empire building, and most of the older judges are not slow to take advantage. They have their own little quirks and eccentricities, which they alone find amusing, and they soon develop a bit of a local reputation. With that comes a variety of sobriquets bestowed upon them by the advocates appearing regularly in front of them, and which aptly describe their less endearing features.

'Penal Pete' describes the judge who hasn't yet discovered the non-custodial sentence, 'Chuckles' the judge who's as miserable as sin, and 'Skippy' the judge who runs into court intent upon setting the all comers record for the fastest jury trial in living memory and who won' t leave even for the eruption of Krakatoa. There are other examples too numerous to mention.

Regardless of their practice in professional life, which was usually undistinguished, when appointed, some circuit judges immediately become the world's greatest experts on the art of advocacy, frequently interrupting or criticising, asking a string of leading questions, and snapping irritably. This can be very distracting for the advocate concerned, and should be stamped on firmly before it gets out of hand.

Other tactics employed by the more boorish of this breed include feigning sleep during the trial, (or in some particularly egregious cases, actually falling asleep), throwing down spectacles or pen with a loud clatter, or breathing heavily like some asthmatic in the middle of an attack.

Robing room gossip should tell you what sort of judge will be trying your case, so that forewarned is forearmed.

THE PART TIMER

The third and last judge you may encounter will be a solicitor or barrister, still in practice, who has agreed to sit as a judge on the less serious cases for a minimum number of days each year. After a careful screening by the Lord Chancellor's department, (part time judges, the suitability of), he will be sent on a course of judicial training. If he keeps his nose clean, and makes all the right noises, he will then be let loose on the unsuspecting public. He will be called a recorder or assistant recorder, and as he will not be inflated with a sense of his own importance, is most agreeable and competent. He will rarely interrupt, is invariably courteous to all and sundry, is usually even handed between prosecution and defence, and makes a very strong case for the abolition of the full time circuit judge.

THE BIT PLAYERS

No roll call would be complete without mentioning the dock officer and the court liaison officer. The dock officer, who works in shifts of ten minutes with his colleagues, is a member of the prison service who sits in the dock with the accused. His main task is to tell the accused when to stand up and when to sit down. Otherwise he takes no further part in the proceedings. It follows that he's a whizz with the *Daily Mirror* crossword!

After ten minutes of sitting aimlessly, he will be relieved by a colleague with the maximum disruption and banging of doors. No judge in his right mind would dream of complaining, so they drift in and out with impunity.

The court liaison officer is a police officer who has forsaken the cut and thrust of street life for the relatively sedentary job of telling the judge all about your client in the event of a conviction. For the rest of the time, he sits at the back of the court doing the *Daily Mirror* crossword!

THE ADVOCATES

Last, and definitely least, is you!

So much for the cast. Now on with the show.

CHAPTER FOUR

The Trial Begins

THE PRELIMINARIES

THE USHER will call on your case, and if you're within earshot, you will enter court with your client lolloping behind you. He will then 'surrender' to the dock officer, and take his seat in the bullpen, otherwise known as the dock. This is a special place reserved exclusively for those accused of crime, and sets them apart from the other participants. Like a caged animal, he is on view for the duration of the trial, and an object of the deepest suspicion and prejudice. If he's not guilty, then what's he doing in there, surrounded by burly men in uniform?

It is unlikely that the judge will be in court when you enter, unless of course it's 'Skippy'. When the court is assembled, the court clerk will direct the usher to fetch the judge from his room, but not before she has taken at least two phone calls, one from her mother who's meeting her for lunch, and the other from the dairy wanting to know how many pints to deliver. These affairs of state take precedence over all other matters, so the court is held in suspended animation whilst she attends to them. When she is ready, and only when, then the usher scuttles off.

The judge enters some seven minutes later, as his room will be at the far end of the building, as planned by the Lord Chancellor's department for maximum efficiency. All stand, with the dock officer propelling the accused to his feet, and then all sit down again.

The court clerk then begins the formal proceedings, unless the phone rings again, in which case play is again suspended until she had answered it.

THE ARRAIGNMENT

This is the moment when the criminal charges, or counts, set out on the charge sheet, or indictment, are read to the accused, and he will be asked if he pleads guilty or not guilty. If the court clerk is newly recruited from the typing pool of the DHSS, she will have an idiot card to guide her through the formalities.

This is always a moment of high drama for the advocate, not so much waiting for the clerk to get it wrong, but waiting for your client to get it wrong. You will have assiduously taken him through the counts on the indictment, explaining them to him in conference, and

taking his clear instructions on each and every matter alleged against him. But many is the time, much to your embarrassment and horror, when your client pleads guilty, because he doesn't understand a word of what is going on, in spite of your best efforts. There are two options available to you in extremis, neither particularly attractive. One is to tell him to watch your head. You will shake it for a not guilty, and nod it for a guilty. The other is to stand next to him in the dock, and do one of those 'watch my lips' routines so beloved of American politicians. Both are demeaning and undignified for the advocate and accused alike, and should be avoided if at all possible. It also confirms in the judge's mind what he's suspected all along, that your client is as guilty as sin, and that the two of you have conspired together to waste a lot of public time and money trying to pull the wool over the jury's eyes. His task, as he sees it, is to thwart you at every turn, and he will strain might and main to do so. Not an auspicious start to an uphill task!

Once the arraignment is over, and your client has finally entered his pleas of not guilty, a jury will be required. A random selection of all those who responded to their jury summons, and who have spent endless hours cooped up in their room, will be hauled up from the catacombs and brought blinking and bewildered into court. They will stand nervously in a tight huddle at the back of the court, until their names are called out, when they will take their seats in the jury box. The clerk will then pick up her next idiot card and address the accused. This may come as a surprise to him if you haven't forewarned him. He will be told, in rather archaic language, that the names he is about to hear are the names of the jurors who will try him. If he objects to them, or any of them, he is to make his objection known when they come to the book to be sworn, and before they are sworn, and his objection shall be heard. This is utter rubbish, and a bygone of yesteryear. The accused has no right to object, and if he accepts the invitation, and objects, he will be told to shut up. It will be your task, as his advocate, to explain all this to him beforehand, and hope he remembers.

The jury will then be empanelled. This means that each juror in turn will take the bible, (or the book, as it is called for no good reason), and swear to try the defendant according to the evidence. Ever since the qualification for jury service was reduced to one of age alone, taking the oath for the illiterate can be something of an ordeal, and the usher may have to help out by intoning the words of the oath for those unable to read. But you, as the advocate, should make a careful mental note of them, and mark them out for special attention. As your client is obviously a moron, it is clearly to his advantage to have a kindred spirit or two on the jury, so that you can ingratiate yourself with them during the trial.

CHAPTER FIVE

The Prosecution Case

THE PROSECUTION OPENING SPEECH

THIS IS ONE of the high points of the prosecution case, before any of their witnesses are called to muddy the waters. The prosecution advocate will outline the case against your client, and in doing so, should pay more than just token lip service to the evidence he will call. You are advised to listen carefully, whilst giving the impression that you are not, in case he lays particular emphasis on a point which you are able to exploit later on. Tactics such as straightening a paper clip, or tearing out several pages from your notebook and numbering them ostentatiously, will help distract the jury, especially as you will be seated right under their noses as convention dictates. Convention also dictates that you should not interrupt your opponent's speech, but there are always exceptions to the rule. If your opponent makes a disparaging remark that is not supported by the evidence, then it is perfectly proper to interrupt with an air of high dudgeon and ask him to refer you to the passage that supports his remark, whilst muttering aloud that his opening speech is supposed to rehearse the evidence he proposes to call, not invent it! This goes down a treat with the jury, and totally wrongfoots your opponent.

THE PROSECUTION EVIDENCE

Once he has completed his opening speech, he will then call his evidence. This takes the form of witnesses taking the oath and telling the jury everything they can remember about the incident which gave rise to your client's arrest. If there has been a considerable lapse of time between arrest and trial, then their evidence becomes a test of memory as much as anything else, although they will have been given their witness statements to read before coming into court. It's a bit like last minute swotting for an exam. The witness is then relieved of his statement, or crib notes, before coming into court, and thereafter he's on his own.

The victim of the crime is usually called first, followed by any other witnesses to the dastardly deed, and then the police officers bringing up the prosecution's rear.

You, as the accused's advocate, will have a copy of each witness statement in front of you as he gives his evidence, and you will be watching, eagle eyed, for any departure from the script. Your opponent's task, rather like the theatrical prompter, will be to keep him on the straight and narrow. If the witness misses out an important piece of evidence, the prosecution advocate will try and reintroduce it. Equally, if the witness gets an important piece of evidence wrong, then your opponent will try and get him to correct it. All this must be done in accordance with the rules. The most important rule when taking a witness through his evidence is never to ask him a leading question. For example, your opponent may ask his witness if there were any identifying features about the man who kicked him in the testicles, but may not ask him if the man who kicked him in the testicles had a thundering great tattoo right in the middle of his forehead. You must be vigilant and ready to leap to your feet, objecting in the strongest possible terms, but in a controlled and measured way. Avoid histrionics, as this will simply alert the otherwise somnolent jury to the very piece of evidence you want them to ignore.

As a general rule of thumb, ask as many leading questions as you think you can get away with, and wait for somebody to object.

You will also discover, at an early stage in the evidence, whether the judge is going to be hostile towards your client or neutral. The occasions when he might actually help your client are so remote they can be effectively discounted.

Remember that if you have got one of those judges who's a self acclaimed expert on advocacy, he will want to take an early part in the proceedings, usually as soon as the first witness has taken the oath. If he is hostile, and the first witness is expected to give particularly damaging evidence against your client, he will interrupt at the outset and tell the witness, in his most charming way, to keep his voice up and direct his answers towards the back row of the jury. If the witness is female, he will invite her to take a seat, and direct the usher to provide her with a glass of water. He will also tell her not to be nervous, and if at any stage she would like a short break from the ordeal about to unfold, then she only has to ask. If the first witness is female and elderly, then the judge might invite her to come and sit next to him on the Bench, so that he can be attentive to her every need.

All this bodes ill for your client, but at least you know what to expect. It will mean that the judge is blatantly hostile, and will do his utmost to defuse any of the explosive and telling points you make during your cross examination. But do not despair. Nobody said it was going to be plain sailing!

Timing is of the essence for the successful defence advocate, and you will have to decide when and how to intervene. The best advice is to play a waiting game. If you jump in too early, it may make the judge all the more determined to tease from the witness the most damaging evidence she is capable of giving, with the worst possible interpretation placed on it against your client. If you hold back, there's an evens chance she will have forgotten most of her evidence, or be hopelessly confused, and the judge's attempts to salvage the wreckage may prove totally

counterproductive. The battle will have been won without a shot being fired, and the only person in court who will fail to be impressed will be your client. This is because most accused, and your client is no exception, will expect their advocate, or 'brief', to be ducking and weaving, bobbing and jabbing, until the witness is reeling on the ropes. It is sometimes a difficult path to tread. Even if your client is found not guilty, he will be singularly unimpressed if you have remained presidentially aloof during his hour of need, and unlikely to use your services again.

After the witness has been taken through her evidence by the prosecution advocate, the judge will plug any gaps as he sees fit. He will do this by asking a string of outrageously leading questions well beyond the scope of any prosecution advocate, and when he gets the answer he wants, he will make a great show of writing it down in his notebook, and reading it back to the witness. Once he has recorded the answer as he would prefer it, he will then make a further great show of underlining it heavily with a large red felt tip pen, and only after he has looked tellingly at the jury, will he allow the next question to be put. All this, of course, is in pursuit of the truth and the interests of that particular brand of justice he has made his own.

There are no hard and fast rules on how to handle a hostile and obnoxious judge, and you will have to proceed as you think best. But there are two overriding considerations when mapping out your game plan. Most jurors had a mother at one time or another, whose memory they cherish, so if you have a mother figure in the witness box, handle her with care, and try and get her on your side. Avoid asking her, therefore, if she would like a cushion, or a new battery for her hearing aid. Those sort of questions go down like a lead balloon. Also remember that the judge will be summing up to the jury, and in the unhappy event of a conviction, will be sentencing your client. He will therefore have the last word, so don't antagonise him needlessly. Having said that, now get stuck in! If the judge is so biassed that not even the most vacant juror can fail to notice, you will get their sympathy vote if nothing else.

Surprising though it may seem, most witnesses other than police officers genuinely try to tell the truth and will usually concede any areas of doubt in their recollection to the benefit of the accused. If you are seen to be treating them fairly, you will achieve as much, if not more, than if you give them a good verbal kicking, and the judge will have less of an excuse for constantly interrupting you. If, in spite of your best efforts, he still interrupts, then immediately resume your seat until he has finished, and remain seated for a few seconds longer to mark your displeasure and to distance yourself from his unwelcome intrusion.

If, against all the odds, you score a significant point in cross examination, then pause, make a conspicuous note of the answer, read it back to the witness to make sure you've got it right, and then underline in heavily with your own red felt tip pen, which should be bigger and squeakier than the judge's. Then thank the witness profusely. Two can play at his game! The judge, of course, will try and get the witness to put a different interpretation on her answer, unfavourable to your client, and may succeed. All the more reason to have your own version faithfully recorded and underlined.

Another useful tip when making a particularly penetrating point, is to turn towards the jury, often with your back to the witness, and repeat the answer you have finally elicited, as if expressly for their benefit, together with appropriate facial contortions for maximum impact. But avoid the habit of some less gifted advocates than yourself, who constantly have their back turned on the witness. Besides looking positively ridiculous, it is downright rude.

So much for the well meaning amateurs. Now on to the professionals.

Police officers invariably make up a significant proportion of the evidence against your client, and they usually play the numbers game. At least six police officers will be ready to testify how they subdued your client against all the odds, another two will interview him and give evidence of full and frank admissions to all the offences with which he is charged, and a few others will give background, but equally damaging, evidence, of your client's propensity to violence and other disagreeable traits.

After the accused has been 'processed' and charged, and either released on bail or remanded in custody, these worthy custodians of law and order will repair to the police canteen, where they will hold a case conference. Over copious cups of tea, their evidence will be choreographed, in the form of witness statements or pocket book entries. Each officer will strive to produce an exact facsimile of his colleague's recollection of events, and commit it to writing.

In police parlance, it is called 'pooling recollections'. Subtlety is not their long suit, and the same phrases and expressions are faithfully reproduced from one version of events to another. You will get six identical accounts of how the accused was seen to be repeatedly kicking the innocent bystander in the testicles, and the time, always 'approximately' 2352 hours, will have been duly noted by all six.

After their notes have been 'made up' together, they will be committed to writing, and not even the wrath of the Almighty will deflect them from their prepared text. They take on the consistency of quick drying cement, and make the ten commandments look like some idle jottings on the back of a fag packet.

Once at court, they will huddle together in the public canteen, reliving the hours they spent together compiling their respective accounts in familiar surroundings, until they have their evidence word perfect. It's a little like some strange Masonic initiation ceremony, where one slip from the prepared text can mean disgrace and ignominy, leading to years of endless toil on the beat, or worse still, the acquittal of the accused.

There is a certain siege mentality amongst police officers which compels them never to break ranks, even in the face of the most glaring inconsistencies in their evidence. They are taught to regard defence advocates as adversaries, and if they agree with any suggestion put to them from that quarter, it is tantamount to committing the eighth deadly sin.

As soon as a police officer has taken the oath, he will immediately ask permission to refer to his pocket book or statement. He will say that he wrote it when the events were still fresh in his memory, and that whilst he may have conferred with his colleagues, he has an independent recollection of all the events recorded in it. Resist the temptation to laugh out loud! The judge will almost always grant permission before you've had a chance to draw breath. This is the cue for the officer to whip out his written account, and read it word for word. When he has finished reciting his litany, it will be your task to cross examine him.

Once you've reconciled yourself to the fact that no police officer worth his pension is going to withdraw one single word of his evidence, you should be able to exploit your adversarial role. You can safely assume that any suggestion you put will be denied. If you suggest to the first witness that your client was drunk, he will immediately deny it. If you suggest the contrary to the second witness, he will immediately tell the jury that the accused was unsteady on his feet, his breath smelt of alcohol, his eyes were glazed, and his speech was slurred. From little acorns, mighty oaks do grow!

In this way, you can chip away patiently at the seemingly impenetrable edifice which confronts you, and who knows, like Samson in the temple of the ungodly, you could bring the whole lot crashing down around their ears.

The interviewing officers can be exposed to the same treatment. If asked the right questions, one might say that the accused was calm and composed at all times, as if grateful for the opportunity of getting the whole thing off his chest. The other may say that he was as nervous as a kitten, exhibiting all the signs of a hunted and cornered animal. All grist to the mill, planting those all important seeds of doubt in the minds of any jurors who might still be listening.

Don't expect the judge to be making a note of your cross examination, especially if it's favourable to the accused. This is where he will be feigning sleep, or constantly interrupting you to enquire if this particular line of questioning is going to help the jury.

There are a variety of tactics which the accomplished advocate can use to embarrass the judge. If he is feigning sleep, then sit down and wait for him to open his eyes. He may ask you if you've finished, whereupon you will immediately rise to your feet and resume your cross examination. If he is making no note at all, then instruct the witness to pause so that the judge can make a careful note of the answer. It can be a slow and painful process, but not for the want of trying.

At the end of the prosecution case, which is usually the high point of the defence case, you will almost certainly want to make a submission.

CHAPTER SIX

Submissions

SUBMISSIONS come under the heading of 'matters of law', which are decided by the judge in the absence of the jury. In reality, all matters, both of law and fact, are decided by the judge, but more of that later.

Matters of law very rarely intrude into a criminal trial, simply because the law is incidental to the proceedings, and is regarded with grave suspicion. These are invariably left to the Court of Appeal to sort out, in their own inimitable way, and a working knowledge of the law is never a consideration high on the list of the Lord Chancellor's department (judges, the suitability of) when appointments are made.

As an advocate practising in the criminal law, you will have equipped yourself with the two current volumes of

Archbold. This is the advocate's bible which, like Topsy, has grown out of all manageable proportions, and can cause severe muscular strain unless handled with care. Its main purpose is to give you something to lean on for maximum gravitas when addressing the jury. It does, however, have another purpose. In it you will find such diverse and illuminating topics as encompassing the carnal knowledge of the heir to the throne (presumably female), obstructing clergymen from celebrating, piracy on the high seas, witchcraft (see under fraudulent mediums) and incorrigible rogues (see also under Judges). All this, of course, is meat and drink to the seasoned advocate, but when making submissions, unless you can refer the judge to the relevant paragraph in Archbold, you can't even begin to interest him.

There are basically two submissions you can make, either that the prosecution have failed to prove a material ingredient of the offence charged, or that their evidence is so unsafe and unsatisfactory that no jury, properly directed, could possibly convict. Most advocates fall back on the second of these propositions, on the basis that it's easier to waffle in high tones of indignation without having to apply any real substance to your argument. It's also good public relations for your client's benefit, and bumps up your legal aid fee by a few pounds, but your chances of success with the judge are negligible. However, if that were a material consideration, then your client would have pleaded guilty at the outset.

Judges do not like submissions, firstly because they are notoriously ignorant of the law, and don't like being reminded of that fact, and secondly, as the accused is patently guilty, the whole exercise is a monstrous waste of public time and money.

There are a number of devices that can be employed by the unsympathetic judge when you announce your intention to raise 'matters of law'. He might tell the jury that this won't take long, and to be back in their places in five minutes. As soon as they've filtered out of court, he will sit back, barely able to disguise his irritation, and glare at you. There are various techniques to put him in his place. The first, and by far the most effective, is to bombard him with a variety of suitable Latin epithets, and a classical education will help enormously. But remember! The exercise cannot be one totally divorced from the evidence, and if challenged, you will have to know what you're talking about. But as very few judges will admit to their own ignorance, you may have him nodding in agreement even though he doesn't understand a word of what you're saying.

You may, for example, begin by telling him that this is clearly a case of 'de minimis non curat lex'. Whilst he's absorbing the enormity of that lofty statement, hit him with 'eodem modo quo quid constituitor, eodem modo destruitor', which, for the philistines amongst you, can be roughly translated as 'the prosecution witnesses haven't come up to snuff'. This is a real show stopper, and should have him reeling and your client nodding with undisguised approval. To put the icing on the cake, tell him that whilst you concede that 'interest reipublicae ne maleficia remaneant impunita' this is clearly a case of 'quod ab initio non valet, in tractu temporis non convalescit'.

All this, of course, will take at least ten minutes, so you've won the first round, with the jury hanging about outside wondering what's going on behind their backs, and impressed by the gravity of it all as one minute succeeds the next. They will become increasingly irritated with the judge, as in the time that elapses as you develop your theme, they could have consumed several cups of poisonous coffee from the vending machine.

For the most part, submissions are simply a rehearsal for your final speech, and their chances of success, particularly in front of a hostile judge, are negligible. But they do serve one important purpose. They help you to gauge the judge's reaction, and could give you some valuable pointers on how to defuse the more outrageous comments he'll be making to the jury when he sums up the case to them. There is also an outside chance that you might wrongfoot him, and in the unhappy event of a conviction, you could always try and work your magic in the Court of Appeal, but don't count on it!

Judges are required, by convention, to hear you out, so you're unlikely to be interrupted. But don't expect a sympathetic hearing. Your judge may show his displeasure by staring fixedly into space, or worse still, at the thundering great tattoo right in the middle of your client's forehead. Alternatively, he might simply inspect his manicure. You should aim for no more than thirty minutes if your submissions are groundless. This will achieve maximum impact with the jury which, after all, is what it's all about.

Your judge might be tempted to give his reasons for

refusing your submissions, but it's unlikely in the extreme. After all, what he says can be used against him in a court of law. So expect him to tell you bluntly that he's against you. But don't let the matter rest there. Ask him to give his reasons 'in case the matter has to be considered elsewhere'. This is shorthand for threatening him with the Court of Appeal, and no judge likes to be challenged in a higher court, especially if that challenge is successful. It doesn't help his career prospects, although the pension remains inviolate, and that is his overriding preoccupation, second only to living long enough to enjoy it. Your tactics will put him on notice as to his future good behaviour.

In the space of thirty minutes of unmitigated waffle, you will have rehearsed your final speech, impressed the socks off the jury, and given the judge a very serious attack of the wobbles. No mean achievement under all the circumstances!

CHAPTER SEVEN

The Defence Case

AT THIS POINT in the trial, a mood of total depression envelops you. You've had fun with the prosecution witnesses, you've rattled the judge and slapped him down a couple of times, and the jury are ready to give you a standing ovation. You've stirred the pot with your submissions, and you're looking good, and feeling good.

The jury filter back into court, parched and bewildered, and you turn towards the dock to contemplate your client. You realise, perhaps for the first time, what a grotesque spectacle confronts you, as he wipes his nose on the back of his hand, drawing attention to the thundering great tattoo right in the middle of his forehead. It's decision time! Do you call him to give evidence, and in the space of a few short minutes, let him undo the minor miracles you've performed on his behalf, or do you persuade him to sit tight, and take his chances?

Your task, as his advocate, is to advise him on the best course of action, which must always stop short of actually telling him what to do. After all, he's the one facing a stiff sentence of imprisonment, not you, and if down he goes, he'll want to leave knowing that he's had his hour in court. This is an important consideration, often overlooked by the most experienced advocates. He may have already made up his mind from the outset to give evidence, in which case there is no need for further discussion. He may also have a posse of equally moronic witnesses he's determined to call, who will dispel any lingering doubts about his guilt which he himself may have failed to achieve. So be it! Every dog must have its day, and who knows, he might surprise you and the jury and give a reasonably convincing account of himself. But don't hold your breath in anticipation!

As his advocate, if you are calling evidence as well as your client, you can if you wish make an opening speech to the jury on his behalf, similar in form and substance to the prosecution opening speech. One word of advice. Don't! Your client will have provided you with a statement setting out his version of events, called a proof of evidence, and you will have conducted the same exercise with any or all of the witnesses he is proposing to call. But it's a racing certainty that their collective evidence will bear little resemblance to their respective proofs, and you run the very grave risk of opening one case, and presenting another totally different one to the jury. This is not only

highly embarrassing, but it also reflects badly on your credibility, as not even the most gullible juror will fail to spot the difference.

The problem with the defence case is that your client will have orchestrated it over copious pints of lager in the Cock and Bull, surrounded by his potential witnesses who, on the evolutionary scale of things, are still in the waiting room of life. This means that whilst they may have mastered the basics of what they are expected to say, there has been little or no fine tuning, and no attempt to prepare them for the rigours of cross examination. To make matters worse, you are not supposed to speak to your client's witnesses once the trial has begun, so there is no opportunity to coach them before they give evidence. You must resign yourself to lots of monosyllabic grunts and furrowed brows as they wage a losing battle with the English language in any intelligible form. The best you can hope for is that they don't actually inflict any terminal damage on the defence case.

Forewarned is forearmed, so you should be under no illusions as you call your client to give evidence.

You announce for the benefit of the judge and jury that you will now call the accused to give evidence, and all eyes turn towards him in anticipation. The judge will immediately put down his pen and sit back, a look of visible hostility across his countenance. This is body language for saying that he doesn't believe a word of what he's about to hear, and sees little point in taking a note of it. The jury will be more open minded about it, but will still eye him with the gravest suspicion as he adopts the gait of

Neanderthal man on his way from the dock to the witness box, escorted by one of the burly men in uniform. Not even the suit and tie, which you insisted he wear for the duration of the trial, can fail to disguise his primordial roots. The thundering great tattoo right in the middle of his forehead will shine out like a beacon in the night, and all this before he's even opened his mouth.

The first hurdle to overcome is the witness oath, when he will swear to tell the truth, the whole truth, and nothing but the truth. If this is his umpteenth appearance in court, he will know it off by heart. He will therefore wave away the card and recite the oath as if it were his favourite party piece. The jury will make a mental note, as your client beams proudly at all and sundry, totally oblivious to this self inflicted wound. If, however, he's relatively new to the experience, then this presents the judge with an early opportunity to put the boot in. As the usher hands the book to the accused, the judge will immediately intervene and ask him if he has any religious beliefs. The accused will stare back, totally mystified, allowing the judge to expose the accused as not only pig ignorant, but also devoid of any love of, or from, the Almighty! He will then instruct the accused to affirm, a form of oath reserved for pagans, devil worshippers and other camp followers. You've lost the first two rounds before he's even given his name and address.

But there's worse to come. If you're particularly unfortunate, your client will be chewing gum, and have his hands firmly thrust into his pockets. The judge will intervene again, and ask the accused if he's masticating.

Your client will immediately remove his hands and reply indignantly that he was only jangling his loose change!

It is now your task to pull him out of the abyss, where the judge has left him clinging by his fingertips, as you attempt to portray him as a witness of truth and the object of a tragic case of mistaken identification.

You should start your examination of the accused by reminding him to keep his voice up when answering questions, and to direct his answers over towards the jury. He will ignore this advice, in spite of several reminders, which can be to your advantage. If the jury can't hear what he's saying, then they can't hold it against him. The judge will almost certainly intervene, yet again, telling him that if he doesn't speak up, he might just as well return to the dock and stop wasting everybody's time.

For what seems like an eternity, you take the accused through his evidence, with little room to improve on the hopeless situation. The best advice is to get it over with as quickly as possible, and try and mop up the mess at the end as best you can.

Cross examination of the accused by your opponent and the judge is invariably another high point in the prosecution case, and the innumerable inadequacies which you've managed to expose during your skillful and incisive questioning of their witnesses are soon forgotten as your client is kicked from pillar to post and back again with unmitigated relish.

You will have told him several times before calling him, to keep his answers short and concise, and not to get into any arguments with the prosecution advocate or the judge.

This is advice which, yet again, he will studiously ignore, as he fights back in the only way he knows how. His performance will be punctuated by gormless smirks towards his friends in the public gallery, who will smirk gormlessly back, further encouraging him in his headlong plunge into the abyss.

The impact which an argumentative and belligerent client may have on the jury is a question of fertile debate. If his antagonists go too far, then his lively ripostes may find some sympathy. It's the Dunkirk spirit, the underdog fighting against insuperable odds, and many's the time when a heavy handed cross examination can produce a wholly negative result, leading to your client's glorious acquittal in the teeth of the evidence. The judge will almost certainly compound the damage, as his large red felt tip pen darts across his notebook like a demented cartographer, underlining the inconsistencies of the accused's lamentable explanations. In these circumstances, there is little point in re-examining your client, and it's best left well alone.

If, however, your opponent deals with the accused in a quiet and measured way, his belligerence will be held against him, and you will have to do your best to repair the damage. Unfortunately, by this time your client will be so fired up that he may not appreciate your helpful and calming influence, and in effect, treat you to more of the same. If this is the case, then drop him like a hot potato, and get him out of the witness box as quickly as possible.

This may be easier said than done, as the judge will be lying in wait, ready to spring one last trap, all in the interests of clarifying the issues for the jury. He will want

to leave a particularly damaging admission ringing in their ears. He may, for example, ask the accused how long he's had that thundering great tattoo right in the middle of his forehead, and exactly what 'Stuff the Pigs' means. He may go on to ask, in all innocence, if your client is a vegetarian, or is he a supporter of animal rights? When your client explains that it's an anti-establishment 'cri de coeur', a careful note will be made that he's against law and order, and out will come the red felt tip pen, squeaking its way across the page.

This places you in a 'Catch 22' situation. If you ask the judge for leave to put further questions in the hope of eliciting a less damaging explanation, he may refuse. If he grants you leave, your client may be too stupid to grasp the lifeline you throw to him, content as he is with the explanation he's already given, and emboldened by the gormless smirks from the public gallery. The best advice is always to deal with as much as possible in your examination in chief, good and bad, in the hope that you will deprive the judge of the sting in the tail.

It is rare in the extreme for your client's witnesses to improve the situation, but if he wants to call them, then call them you must. It is very frustrating for the skilled and experienced advocate to watch his case go from bad to worse, but you must grin and bear it.

If at all possible, try and end your ordeal on a high note. This can be achieved by calling a character witness, preferably a bishop or a titled pillar of society, who will speak of your client's charitable works or his selfless devotion to a variety of worthy causes, but it has to be admitted, the chances of finding such a nugget of gold in an otherwise barren wasteland are remote in the extreme, and you may have to settle for the landlord of the Cock and Bull telling the jury that he once saw the accused put 10p in the Guide Dogs for the Blind box. Hopefully, he will omit to say that the accused was so drunk at the time, he didn't know what he was doing, and when he sobered up, he demanded his 10p back.

CHAPTER EIGHT

Final Speeches

SO THERE you have it! You have presented your case, such as it is, and your last witness marks the conclusion of the evidence. It is time for final speeches, where each side tries to persuade the jury of the accused's guilt, or innocence, as the case may be.

The prosecution advocate goes first, and there are two schools of thought about his role in the proceedings, and the way in which he should summarise his case to the jury. The first casts him in the role of a 'soi-disant' minister of justice, placing the evidence fairly and impartially before them, and inviting them to convict only if they are satisfied so that they feel sure of guilt. His is not an adversarial role, nor should he strive to secure a conviction in any event. But there are two gremlins perched on his shoulder which militate against this approach, no matter how laudable. They are the CPS and the judge. The CPS clerk, who sits behind the advocate when she isn't busy reporting back to the 'vetting solicitor' on his progress and general aptitude, has a check list in front of her to rate his performance. This list will be used to assess his future usefulness to the Service, and contains no reference to fairness and impartiality. The prosecution advocate is expected, by those who pull his strings, to be combative, aggressive, unyielding and merciless in his conduct of the case, as he wields the sword of justice to strike down the ungodly, and who more ungodly than the moron with the thundering great tattoo right in the middle of his forehead! And besides, if he's not guilty, then what's he doing sitting in the dock surrounded by burly men in uniform?

The judge also has a vested interest in the proceedings. As he is supposed to be impartial, it looks bad form if he is seen to be more combative, aggressive, unyielding and merciless in his conduct of the case than the party charged with the responsibility of proving the guilt of the accused, and this can sometimes lead to a serious miscarriage of justice when the accused is found not guilty. The judge will prefer to give the appearance of riding along on the prosecution's coat tails, and not the other way round, otherwise it reflects badly on the dignity of his office and a proper sense of his own importance.

Expect therefore, a thunderous speech from the prosecution about the jury's duty to convict, given the overwhelming evidence against the accused. He will conveniently forget all the loopholes in his own case, and concentrate upon the unsatisfactory evidence called by the defence. And let's face it, who can blame him? After all, you've given him enough ammunition to start the third world war.

Tactics here are vital, given the convention that you do not interrupt your opponent's final speech. But bear in mind the biblical saying about eyes and teeth. Your speech follows his!

The most important tactic is one of timing. You will know by now what time the court usually adjourns for the day, so you will have orchestrated your case to finish with just about half an hour to go. This means that your opponent will be called upon to make his final speech at the end of the day, when the jury are at their least receptive, and anxious to get home. The time factor will act as an additional constraint, as he will feel under pressure to finish at the appointed hour. This means that he will have to hurry his speech, with no time for flowery exhortations or perorations. This tactic gives you the added advantage of addressing the jury first thing in the morning, when they will be at their most attentive, and will have forgotten every word of your opponent's speech.

Other tactics commend themselves, and can be used at your discretion. You can, for instance, arrange for one or two accomplices in the public gallery to leave and return as ostentatiously and noisily as the proceedings will allow, but on a given signal, such as removing your wig and inspecting the various life forms within. As your opponent is about to reach the high point of his speech, get your clerk to leave court on the pretext of fetching something for you from the robing room, and make sure he leaves and returns in the half crouch position. This passable impersonation of Quasimodo will be immediately noticed by all except your opponent, who will have his back to you. He will be aware of something going on, as all eyes turn to watch the hunchback of Notre Dame, but he will be helpless to intervene, and has no alternative but to soldier on.

The judge, of course, will notice little of this gamesmanship, as he will be busily taking a verbatim note of the prosecution speech to weave into his summing up, and his head will be buried in his book. You, however, should avoid the temptation to do the same, as if the jury see you busy scribbling away, they might think it's important, and start paying attention. Your clerk can take a discreet note if you think it might help, and you've got overnight to put your thoughts in order.

Finally, his speech over, the prosecution advocate will sink into his seat, drained of all emotion, and, feeling cheated of his finest hour, or half hour, as the case may be, will glance nervously at the CPS clerk for her approbation. She, for her part, will be busy filling in his score card on a scale of one to ten.

The day dawns bright as you prepare for your finest hour. You will dress conservatively, avoiding any distracting appendages such as a brightly coloured pocket handkerchief or gold fob and chain. Wear your darkest suit with the subtle pin stripe, and not the one you foolishly bought in the sales which makes you look like a bookmaker's runner. You want the jury to concentrate on you, and not on your apparel.

You will have put the finishing touches to your speech the night before, but avoid the temptation to write it out word for word. This will destroy your spontaneity, which is essential if you are to rubbish the prosecution case successfully. Use headings, numbered in chronological order, and set yourself a time limit.

Once at court, you will want to go into retreat to avoid any unnecessary distractions. Explain this to your client, otherwise he may misinterpret your remoteness, and he's got enough to depress him as it is. Permit yourself one cup of strong black coffee, but no more. Incontinence is not conducive to quiet, reasoned, argument. Go to the lavatory just before you go into court, and make sure you do up your zip afterwards.

A final speech to the jury is no different in technique to any public speech, except that you have a captive audience who are not expected to barrack or fall asleep. If a member of the jury does fall asleep, then you are doomed, and you have only yourself to blame.

At last the waiting is over, and the appointed hour is upon you. The court has assembled, and twelve eager faces turn expectantly towards you, like empty vessels waiting to be filled, or so you hope.

The first and most important thing to remember is that the judge will be doing his level best to contradict each and every point you will be making on behalf of the accused, so you will have to say something to prepare the jury for this eventuality. By now, hopefully, they will have realised where the judge's sympathies lie, and may take his blandishments with a pinch of salt. But contrary to popular myth, the jury do have minds of their own, and once incarcerated in their retiring room, you have no control over their deliberations, nor do you know for sure which way they will jump. You will have had some inkling during the trial from their expressions and from the occasional aside comment which you may have overheard, but up to the point when they actually retire, they have little idea why they've been dragged from home and work to sit mute, bored and uncomfortable when they could be doing better things.

Now is the time to enlighten them. Explain to them patiently and sympathetically that they are the sole judges of the facts in this case, not you, not the prosecution advocate, and certainly not the judge, and on this, if nothing else, you and the judge are in entire agreement. As the judge is obliged to explain this to the jury in due course, you are on safe ground, and cannot be criticised. This point must be laboured time and time again, because some juries, particularly in the shire counties, mistakenly believe they should convict the accused simply to please the judge. This is perfectly understandable, given the pomp and circumstance which surrounds the judge and the reverential air of the courtroom drama as it unfolds before them. He sits alone on an elevated dais, wearing those absurdly garish robes, everybody stands when he enters and leaves court, the advocates and other court officials bow and scrape, and he is addressed as 'Your Honour'.

This whole performance lends a certain aura to his role in the proceedings which is often misplaced and frequently misunderstood. It is your task to bring the jury down to earth. But beware! Some judges, particularly the pompous and self important variety, can be very prickly about criticism, so you must veil your remarks in coded form. The negative form is the most effective. You can tell the jury, when dealing with the judge's role in the proceedings, that they may have formed a view as to where his sympathies lie, but far be it from you to suggest that the judge has been anything other than fair and impartial throughout the trial, and that his helpful interventions, frequent though they may have been, were intended simply to clarify the issues for their benefit. Even the most catatonic jury cannot fail to receive that particular coded message loud and clear. Constant references in this vein will help you to drive the point home, and may eventually persuade the jury that they can, if they wish, decide the case for themselves.

The rest of your speech, in both content and style, is a matter for your own personal judgment, but the structure follows that of any successful speech. Start if you can with some sort of anecdote, to capture the jury's attention and to soften the impact of the serious stuff to follow. The 'picture if you will' approach is a tried and tested opening formula, and used by some of the best advocates in the business.

Rubbishing the prosecution case is also fair game. The defence case is best left well alone, given the shallow and infertile ground on which it was nurtured, and you certainly don't want to remind the jury of any part of it. Rubbishing the accused as a low life specimen of humanity with a brain the size of a pinhead is bad form, and may elicit a burst of outraged indignation from the dock. That would be an unwelcome distraction, to be discouraged at all costs.

Whilst you should range across the whole of the jury when addressing them, as nobody wants to feel left out, concentrate your most telling remarks on those members of the jury who appear the most receptive, as you'll need all the help you can get when they retire to consider their verdict. Watch out for the occasional nod, or the sympathetic smile, and home in. It's called 'working your audience'.

Convention forbids you from mentioning the gravity of the offence or the likely consequences of a conviction in the hope of getting a sympathy verdict. Besides which, after your client's performance and those of his witnesses, sympathy in that department is going to be hard to find.

If possible, and it's remote in the extreme, leave them wanting more, so never go on too long, and avoid needless repetition.

Finally, and most important of all, you must end on a high note. The 'hand on the heart' finale is a popular one, his 'life in your hands' approach, tugging at their raw emotions, inviting the jury to overlook the overwhelming evidence against your client and concentrate instead upon this unloved and vilified human being, friendless and abandoned, who cries out to them in his hour of need, to end his ordeal and release him from the chains that bind him! Heady stuff, and not a dry eye in the house!

CHAPTER NINE

The Summing Up

THIS IS THE most frustrating part of the trial from your point of view, for reasons that should now be clear. The judge, by his standards at least, has held back from commenting on the evidence, and has had to sit and listen with growing impatience as the case has unfolded. He has, of course, tried to steer it along the proper path, and you have already referred to his 'helpful' interventions. But now, at last, he has centre stage, the spotlight is upon him, and he's not going to exit until he's made it abundantly clear to the jury that it's their duty to convict, and any other verdict would be taken as a personal insult.

The judge's summing up falls into two distinct parts. The first deals with directions on the law. He will remind the jury that they are the sole judges of fact, that the evidence is for them, and them alone, and that if he should comment on the evidence in the course of his summing up, whilst such comments are intended to be helpful, they are free to accept or reject them as they see fit. Of course the judge means nothing of the sort, and woe betide a jury which does not accept his interpretation of the evidence!

He is also obliged to tell the jury that they can only convict the moron with the thundering great tattoo right in the middle of his forehead, only if they are satisfied so that they feel sure of his guilt. He will then go on to explain exactly why they can, and should. This is called redressing the balance.

His final direction on the law is an explanation of the offence itself, couched in long and windy legal jargonese, and will be totally incomprehensible. However, as has been observed elsewhere, the law seldom intrudes into a criminal trial, and should not be allowed to trouble the jury.

After these opening remarks and directions, the judge will then embark upon the real purpose of the summing up. Over the next hour or two, he will analyse the salient features of the evidence, as he sees them, and explain why the evidence is overwhelmingly in favour of a conviction. This is done by the use of the phrase 'you may think'. This is a euphemism for 'I think, and so should you!' In this helpful and impartial way, the judge ploughs through the evidence in a monotonous regurgitation, laying particular emphasis on the passages he has laboriously underlined. The one good thing from your point of view is that the jury is invariably bored rigid, and the longer he goes on, the quicker they switch off.

Although you are powerless to intervene during the summing up itself, unless the judge goes totally off the rails, there are certain tactics you can employ to soften the impact.

The first, and most obvious one, is the same tactic you used on the prosecution advocate when forcing him to make his closing speech at the end of the day's proceedings. As you will have begun your final speech at the beginning of the following morning, your timing must take into account the anticipated length of the judge's summing up. No judge likes to send a jury out to consider their verdict after three in the afternoon at the latest, otherwise the Civil Service, in the form of the clerk, the ushers, and the dock officers, will come down on him like a ton of bricks. There is always a risk that the jury's deliberations will take them well beyond the close of the day's business, and that is to be deplored. If you can time your speech so that the judge cannot finish his summing up and send the jury out, it means that he will have to conclude his summing up and send them out first thing the next morning. This will give them the chance to forget almost everything he's said to them. So timing is absolutely vital! If you end your speech too soon, it will give him the time to send the jury out with his concluding remarks ringing in their ears. If you go on too long, he will complete the bulk of his summing up the next morning, and you will have lost the initiative.

Another tactic worthy of consideration, also employed during your opponent's speech, is a visit to the lavatory by your client at an appropriate point in the summing up, again by prearranged signal. This performance will require him to speak to the dock officer in a stage whisper, who will then call your clerk over, again in a stage whisper. Your clerk will then relay the request to you, again in a stage whisper, and you will then rise to your feet. Apologise profusely for interrupting, and pass the message on, indicating at the same time that you have no objection to the judge continuing his summing up in the accused's absence. This is vital as you will want him to disrupt the summing up on his return, and it's no good if the judge stops and waits for your client to relieve himself. However, just in case he does, make sure that the accused takes at least ten minutes to perform the act of nature, real or imagined, so that the jury will be concentrating upon his impending return, and not on what the judge was belabouring at the time. In these circumstances, a minute can seem like an hour, and the judge will have lost the train of his thoughts and the jury's undivided attention.

It is regarded as discourteous and unprofessional to cough and splutter at his more outrageous remarks, or to draw your breath in sharply and turn your eyes heavenwards, from whence your client's salvation may yet come. You must remain equanimious in the face of the gravest provocation.

One final tactic is worthy of consideration. It's called the 'ringing in the ears' backflip. The judge will usually reserve his most stinging remark to the end of his summing up, with a parting 'you may think' ringing in the ears of the jury as he sends them off to convict. Just before the jury bailiff takes the oath and leads them away, you must intervene. Think of a particular piece of evidence favourable to the accused, and there can't be that many, which the judge has studiously ignored. Begin by complimenting the judge on his fair and balanced summary of the evidence, and then ask him, in your most charming voice, if he would care to remind the jury of it, as you assume his failure to do so was an oversight which he would welcome the opportunity of putting right.

He will of course, do no such thing, and will snap back that his summary of the evidence was of necessity selective. You will smile indulgently, and resume your seat. This tactic has the obvious advantage of leaving a particularly favourable piece of evidence ringing in the jury's ears, and you have to a large extent cancelled out the judge's final remark. Game and set to you, with the match yet to be decided!

After the jury bailiff has taken the oath to keep the jury in some private and convenient place, and not to suffer anybody to talk to them concerning the trial here this day, unless it be with the leave of the court, she will lead the jury off to their retiring room like some mother hen, chatting to them as they go. She will also take any exhibits with her, and generally settle the jury down in their room.

Now the waiting begins, and the first asinine question your client will ask you is how long the jury will be out. Take a few minutes to reassure him about the trial, and try and be positive. There is little point in telling him that if the jury believe his evidence, they'll believe anything. Better to tell him that he has placed all the material issues squarely before the jury, and they will doubtless be giving them their careful consideration. This is the sort of pompous remark your client expects you to say, although he won't understand a word of it. Thereafter, you can studiously ignore him until the jury return with their verdict.

The way in which the jury reaches its verdict is one of the great mysteries of life, and no advocate can be privy to their discussions. But robing room gossip gives a valuable insight into their approach, culled from loquacious jury bailiffs and the occasional friend who has been called to jury service.

The first ten minutes are usually occupied by a lively debate on which of their number is going to be the foreman. This is a grave responsibility, as the foreman is supposed to chair the discussions and deliver the verdict when they return to court. Most jurors shy away from the task, but occasionally there will be two or three who fancy the job, and an unseemly squabble will ensue. When at last it has been resolved, only then will they begin their deliberations.

Juries usually split into three distinct camps. The first camp, consisting of the better educated middle class members, will want to apply the law as directed by the judge, and review the evidence in detail in accordance with their oath. The foreman will almost certainly be chosen from this group.

The second camp, consisting of honest sons and daughters of toil, will have made up their minds a long time ago, either because of the thundering great tattoo right in the middle of the accused's forehead, or because they refuse to believe the police on principle, and regard any meaningful discussion as a complete waste of time.

The third camp consists of the floating voters, who will

take no part in the discussions and simply vote with the majority for a quiet life, in the hope that nobody will ask them to give their reasons. It is a source of great wonder that from such a socially diverse and potentially divided group of individuals comes forth a measure of unanimity.

THE VERDICT

Once the jury has reached their verdict, they will knock on their door to alert the jury bailiff. She will then scurry off to the court clerk with the news.

At last the waiting is over, and the adrenalin begins to pump. The tension is almost unbearable as you and your client troop into court, and the jury file in. You deliberately avoid catching their eye as you try to look busy and at the same time, casually unconcerned. Your pulse begins to race, and your heart pounds, as you wonder if you've pulled it off. A few seconds delay as the court clerk flicks through her idiot cards to find the right one. She asks the foreman if they've reached a verdict on which they are all agreed. He says yes. And now the moment of truth, the moment you've all been waiting for ;

"Members of the jury, do you find the defendant guilty or not guilty as charged?"

A momentary pause which seems to last for ever

"Not guilty."

There are audible gasps of astonishment from the accused and the public gallery, as the judge throws his head back in disbelief. In the best traditions of public service for little reward, you show no emotion. And then all hell breaks loose, as papers are thrown in the air, spontaneous applause and cheering fills the court as the judge marches out angrily to lick his wounds, your client leaps from the dock, and almost sobbing with emotion, embraces you in gratitude. He and his friends then lift you shoulder high and chair you out of court as the jury burst into a hearty rendition of 'For he's a jolly good fellow.' Total strangers approach you with their congratulations, and the local press crowd round you for a few well chosen comments. And then you wake up.

"Guilty," intones the foreman of the jury.

There is always a sense of disappointment, and even though you hoped against hope that the day could be won against all odds, there is relief that your ordeal is nearly over, and resignation to the inevitable.

CHAPTER TEN

Sentence

THE PROSECUTION advocate, relieved and assured of at least one more brief, now calls the court liaison officer to tell the judge all about your client. This is the part which both the prosecution and judge particularly enjoy, because it tells the jury that the accused is an unmitigated villain with a string of previous convictions for similar offences, and they can rest easy in their beds knowing they've brought in the right verdict.

MITIGATION

This is the speech you will make pleading clemency for your client before he is sentenced. In some cases, admittedly few in number, your persuasive skills can make a difference to sentence, but this is not one. The judge will have already made up his mind, probably before the trial began, so what you say will be for your client's ears only. He will expect you to say nice things about him, and this won't be easy. You can't make it up as you go along, so you will have very limited material at your disposal. The judge, for his part, will either be studying that very nasty stain on the ceiling above his head, or inspecting his manicure, or worse still, checking the maximum sentence he is allowed to pass in his copy of Archbold, turning the pages ostentatiously for dramatic effect. There is nothing the advocate can do in the face of such discourtesy, and to ask him if he would like you to pause while he composes himself will add another six months to your client's sentence. The judge is getting his own back, and loving every minute of it.

You may have the benefit of a report from the Probation Service, but it is unlikely in the extreme. If you do, it will contain a reasonably detailed account of your client's miserable childhood, and equally miserable adolescence, and a halfhearted recommendation for community service, which the judge will ignore. But you may be able to extract a nugget or two from the report, which you can weave into your submissions.

The best speeches in mitigation follow a fairly standard format. You should begin with the time honoured expression that the accused is bound by the verdict of the jury, just as you are bound by your instructions. This is a pompous way of saying that everybody knew he was guilty from the outset, but you're buggered if you're going to admit it now. No need to say anything more about the offence, it will only make matters worse.

Many advocates keep a check list of standard mitigating factors, which you should number as appropriate. Set out below are some of the more tried and tested ones, in no particular order of importance:

The accused has a pregnant girlfriend, preferably from one of the ethnic minorities. She has been sitting in court throughout the trial, and her unborn child cries out for clemency. The accused is her sole means of support, both financially and emotionally, and a sentence of imprisonment will place great strains upon the already fragile relationship, which may not survive the enforced separation. The fact that the accused has been unemployed for as long as he can remember and spends all his dole money on copious quantities of drink may not escape the judge's attention.

The accused has a job waiting for him as soon as he leaves court—this of course stretches belief to breaking point, particularly as he will have nothing in writing, and will be inviting the judge to take it at face value. As the judge will have decided long ago that the accused wouldn't know the truth if it jumped up and grabbed him by the throat, this submission will have no appeal whatsoever.

The accused has been out of trouble for the past X weeks/months/years—again, not much mileage here, especially if he has a string of previous convictions going back to prepubescence.

The accused has bad an unhappy childhood, and is the product of a broken home—the same can be said of millions of others who don't go around kicking the living daylights out of anything that moves.

The accused has an artistic bent, as evidenced by the thundering great tattoo right in the middle of his forehead—unhelpful in the extreme, and counterproductive!

This list does not claim to be exhaustive, but should give you a few useful ideas on how to soften the blow of the punitive sentence of imprisonment which the judge has in mind, and which will leave your client gaping in disbelief.

There are other submissions of general application which can be woven into your mitigation regardless of the circumstances. They can be summarised as follows:

Standing at the crossroads of life—

A real determination to keep out of further trouble—

Coming to terms with his excessive drinking habits—

The interests of justice must be balanced with the interests of the accused—

Light at the end of the tunnel—

Imprisonment will sharpen his criminal proclivities, rather than diminish them—

Finally, finish your mitigation with the lofty phrase that if imprisonment is inevitable, then such a sentence should be as short as is consistent with the judge's public duty. That said, you have said it all.

SENTENCE

This is the moment the judge has been savouring from the moment he first walked into court at the beginning of the trial, and he will have been rehearsing a string of acid remarks to direct at your client.

If the accused has been tried at the Old Bailey before one of the more crusty octogenarian judges who are wheeled out of retirement from time to time, the clerk of the court may rise with the appropriate idiot card and deliver the following incantation:

Prisoner at the bar, you have been convicted of crime. Have you anything to say before sentence is passed?

It is unlikely you will have alerted your client to this particular anachronism, and he may be wondering why he bought a dog if he is being invited to bark himself. As you will have already said everything possible on his behalf, and he's got nothing to lose, he will probably reply in time honoured fashion that he's got sod all to say. The judge, who is deaf, will ask the clerk what the accused said. The clerk will tell the judge that the accused has sod all to say, and the judge will express surprise, as he could have sworn he saw his lips move.

In his sentencing remarks, the judge will begin by congratulating the jury on their verdict, based as it was on overwhelming evidence of guilt, and will reprimand the accused for wasting public time and money. He should eschew gratuitously offensive remarks about the accused being a revolting little moron without any shred of decency, as height, or lack of it, and intellectual vacuity, should form no part of the sentencing procedure. He may remark that he has listened carefully to everything that has been urged on the accused's behalf, which is a polite way of saying that he has listened and paid no regard whatsoever to the mitigation. If the judge tells the accused that he has listened carefully to everything which has been so ably urged on his behalf, this means that he hasn't listened at all. The advocate's ability, for these purposes, is in inverse proportion to impact.

After sentence has been passed, the accused is removed from the dock and down to the cells as quickly as possible, to discourage him from any incisive comments about the judge's progeny. Once departed, the judge will then fawn all over the jury, thanking them effusively for the careful attention they gave to the evidence, and for the exemplary way in which they discharged their public duty. These comments are reserved only for guilty verdicts.

THE POST MORTEM

Before you leave court to fight another day, you must go and see your client in the cells. First, however, there is the grieving girlfriend to console, her tear stained face looking expectantly towards you for comfort and reassurance.

In the newer courts, the cells have been renamed the custody suite. A handwritten notice by the bell warns you against pressing it more than once, on pain of incurring the wrath of the prison service. You will have to wait anything between five and fifteen minutes before the door

CUSTODY SUITE
RING
ONCE
ONLY

is opened, depending on the time of day. If your visit coincides with one of the recognised breaks as laid down in the union manual, then you may be advised to take sandwiches and coffee with you. Eventually, with much ceremony and clanking of keys, the hatch in the door is opened and a face stares at you for a minute or two, sizing you up like some freak attraction in a peep show.

There are two questions your client will ask you. What are his chances on appeal, and how long will he have to serve with time off for good behaviour? The answer to the second question is best approached with the help of a calculator. The answer to the first is usually none.

The visit to the custody suite is invariably an uncomfortable one for the advocate, as there is nothing you can say that your client wants to hear. Telling him you gave it your best shot sounds unconvincing in the circumstances, and will do little to reassure him. He won't be in the best frame of mind to appreciate your undoubted skills as an advocate, let alone dwell on them, and this is not the time to look for gratitude. The best approach is to tell him that you will give careful consideration to the trial and sentence, and let him know. As the two of you sit there in moody silence, you must look for a way of withdrawing gracefully. The promise of an imminent visit from his girlfriend is usually a bestseller, as he would rather be chatting to her than to you. You slide away with a cheery farewell, but avoid the parting remark that you'll see him soon, as this could be misinterpreted.

And so you emerge from the depths out into the bright sunlight, and on to greater glory. Not for you the prison bars, where no light shines and no sweet flowers bloom. Not for you the stench of urine, the lament of despair, the soulless surroundings devoid of hope and dignity. But no matter how helpless you may feel, you can be comforted in the knowledge that you did your best. For a few short hours you strode a small corner of the stage of life, and you strode it like a Colossus.